NO MATTER HOW DARK THE STAIN

POEMS AND INSPIRATION FOR THE WOMAN IN PAIN

ANDREA LYNN WEHLANN

Copyright @2021 Andrea Lynn Wehlann.

All rights reserved in all countries.

Published by Ingenium Books Publishing Inc.

Toronto, Ontario, Canada M6P 1Z2

ingeniumbooks.com

Ingenium Books supports copyright. Copyright fuels innovation and creativity, encourages diverse voices, promotes free speech, and helps create vibrant culture. Thank you for purchasing an authorized edition of this book and for complying with copyright laws by not reproducing, scanning, or distributing this book or any part of it without permission. You are supporting writers and helping ensure Ingenium Books can continue to publish nonfiction books for readers like you. You are permitted to excerpt brief quotations in a review.

ISBNs

Paperback 978-1-989059-73-9

eBook 978-1-989059-74-6

Epigraph: Anne Carson, award-winning author, poet, literature professor, from an interview in The Paris Review: Anne Carson, The Art of Poetry No. 88, Issue 171, Fall 2004, page 8 of 30.

For N, L, A, and 7 stars.

/MƏˈMĒSIS/

Greek for "imitation"

Plato's theory of *mimesis* was that all forms of art are imitation: of life, of an idea, of reality.

Mimesis allows us to explore the relationship with our inner selves, our emotions, beyond what's possible in the real world.

In poetry, a form of *mimesis*, the words are written at one point in time, read at another point in time, and through this mind-to-mind and heart-to-heart experience, the reader finds that she is / they are transformed.

NO MATTER HOW DARK THE STAIN

Healing can happen in an instant. Opening this book is like opening your awareness. It's the first step in the direction of love, of listening to your heart.

You are not defined by what happened to you. You are what you do in this moment.

You may feel misunderstood, different, broken, unloved, or lonely. Or you may remember a time when you felt this way.

We are not schizophrenic, depressed, drunk, addicted, abused, or victims. We are love. We see and attract the good and we evolve to our potential. We do this through visualization and by remembering our true nature. We do this by taking steps to embrace where we are, as all we need is already within.

Where there is light, there can be no darkness. Love is like a switch that heals our darkness.

I want to help you see that you have what you need. Here's a hint at how I've organized the poems and inspiration for your journey.

Section one, *Innocence*, contains the poetry that represents and reflects on the times I was hopeful, wistful, and before my biggest hurts.

You may need to approach section two, *That's the Thing About the Heart, It Breaks*, when you're ready to embrace the tough stuff. These poems flung themselves into consciousness as a way to help me heal from abuse, including rape. There is darkness here.

Section three, *Rise of the Goddess*, shows my journey into the light, my healing, and is where you can find your own path to peace, no matter how dark the stain of your pain.

I've opened my heart. Felt the pieces falling apart. Glued them together, on my knees, piece by piece. I tell my yoga students, "That's the thing about the heart. It breaks."

Healing can happen in an instant. I am holding space for your pain and I want my words to be your light. Your body wants to heal. Feed it with these words. Close your eyes, breathe them in, into that space we are all open, free, and interconnected.

You are not alone and you can do this—as I have. You're a star. It's never too late to shine. Thank you for taking this journey into the light with me. I hope you enjoy my poetry in *No Matter How Dark the Stain*.

Andrea

INNOCENCE

PART ONE

SAND FOUNDATIONS

no more sand foundations
fear, secrets, or lies
destroy the destroyers in your mind
seek the hidden
subconscious stories
patterns and darkness
become aware
flick the switch
shine the light
ease the flame
into good days and good ways
good patterns and good returns
kindness flows within you
no more sand foundations

SURFING ON DREAMS

surreal
closing the gap of light and dark
trapped
flooding upstream
flushing and healing
what clings to our dreams
we can see
closing the gap of light and dark
surfing
on dreams once carved in stone

BRIEF BEAUTY

beautiful rainbow
bold and strong and lean
booming bright
between waterfall
and daylight
beautiful rainbow
being as you are
we look forward to
your strength and colour
to wipe our tears at night
burst of beauty
shaped and strong
being where you are
knowing where to be
your brief beauty
lights the colour in me

THE TASTE OF BERRIES

the taste of berries
never quench your thirst
like truth
truth
the tidal wave of condemnation
stirring beneath your soul
a thunderstorm
of lightning
furious floods
flowing choices
belief we burn into ashes
wisdom lights the knowing

TRUTH IS ALL

learning every moment
maybe trying too hard
or wanting too fast
journey
journey
no destination

here and now
or now and here
truth is all

shady days
grey skies
endless emotions
waters rise

catching songs and singing birds
stealing kisses
loving words

grey and blue
black and white
colours fade
light is light

awakened on the devil's ground
wings have grown beyond profound
to lift in flight
sunsets, horizons, enjoy the ride

truth is all
we see inside

rain washed days
or pictures hung
life is for enjoying
it has already begun

truth is all

DISTANT DREAMS

under the feathers
claws of your strength
surrendering
i walk the plank

i see no words
illusions veil
catch a whiff
on the strongest winds

left transcended
weight without sin
fresh plantation
strength within
prying eyes begin again

gentle escapes
wisps away
freedoms face
washed away

blinding tears
thoughts disappear
a lonely lead
starring role
victims' virtue
control
control

CLEAR THE VIEW

i take a deep breath to clear the view
times i wished yet seldom knew
a day is long and night so near
a silhouette scared and haunted with fear

some part aware with vision clear
thumping inward and drawing near
racket so loud it shutters the pain
with endless tears we only gain

magic of the wizard unknown
felt between each fragile bone
ragged edge of sweetened steam
a swift current burning through the stream

naked eyes so precious to glare
beneath the lion's piercing stare
i take a deep breath to clear the view
times i wish someone else knew

desperate earth the training ground
innocence lost and justice found
between rare bursts of the frigid seam
i take a deep breath while living its dream

HERE WITH ME

you are here with me
i closed my eyes
i saw the light
felt your arms caress my sides
my cheeks could not help the stretch
i felt blessed as i smiled
i miss you so much
i feel so peaceful
the most precious gift
i am lucky to have your touch
as i miss you so much
thank you for the moment
i felt you here with me
i feel no limitations
i feel you
here with me

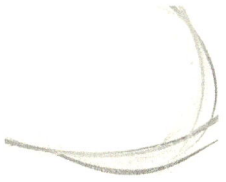

WANDER THE SWAMP

funny how the day burns
in sweet kisses
never stolen from beyond
beyond the banks in bloom of fear
trenches dug with deep despair
liquid eyes embrace the freedom
hindered upon your lovers' glare
believe deception's smile
i wander the swamp all the while
falling on bent knees
chains holding each wrist
i see the eyes i loved
i see the lips once kissed
darkness covets my flesh
once again i sink
muddy waters too thick
no weight to stand
God bless me as i fall
God bless me to rise again

POWDER

i sit with my powdered face
i can
watch it melt away
easily it fades

i watch the white
and green
as it runneth over with red
i see through
and feel the dead

i sit with my powdered face
watch it melt away
i can
take the powder in its rightful voice
and contain its presence
reveal the inner beauty
so often unnoticed
dress with powder
play its game
covet only truth
i can
undress and expose naked

the raw innocence and purity
of only universe
given within us
from only our divine
our love

INFINITY

conformity is fraud
powers self contained
smiles comfort horrors
while miles left to gain
hearts the desperate search
their powers self contained
gorillas in the mist
while miles left to gain

the soul covets the self
powers self contained
endless search for truth
while miles left to gain

beauty in the eyes
their powers self contained
beholders hypnotize
while miles left to gain

tortured feet on burnt cement
miles left to gain
journeys never cease
but the power we contain

I HAD AN IMAGE ONCE

when a girl is young, delicate and sincere
she dreams of a man
perfect in every sense
beautiful
impossible to find

i had an image once
created with love, precision and care
someone to fulfill my dreams
miraculous reality

i had an image once
of love so deep
no other could compare
mutual understanding
strong and lasting
contained yet uncontrollable passion
we'd feel each other's bodies
burning to be together forever

i had an image once
it became true
i needed that image once
now i need you

ONE DAY

the water runs without our control
controlled by one we'll one day know
and though it runs
kills without regret
one day we'll see
it washes away
the hurt of mostly death
the one that means the most
although we cannot know
one day we'll meet the water
and the wet
it spills over
to anoint our fellow being
one day we'll meet the water
one day we'll kiss the sky

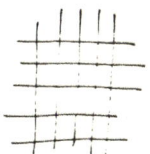

YOUNG GUNS

young guns collide
with youth and rage
the incessant plot
of teach and taught
is lost between your knowledgeable rot
you twist and bite
in dangerous extremes
wallowing in words
soliciting dreams
time will turn your page
drop your anger
lose your rage
heal the brand you choose to fight

steer your raft
in the ocean's hiss
feel the God in each wave's kiss
open the chest
to the mind within
see each heart
lose visions of sin

here is the peace you long to ignore
here in the channels of earth meets shore
explore the tides and wet the will
see results and live the thrill
ponder the breath each splash will bring
burst it apart and feel the sting
enchanting it is
between your toes
enchanting to live as nobody knows
purity of thought
destiny will attain
through lives of work
surrender and gain
forfeit the prize and reap the rewards
taste the flavour
genuine terms
live in the mercy
of no more words

DEATH INTERCEDES

crystallized visions
depth beyond
palpable flavours
sweet harmony

death intercedes
bodies engage
brittle and frail
strong rampage

solitude heightens
beauty peels
frowning faces
death intercedes

withering humans
depth beyond
crystallized visions
death intercedes

underground beats
smile covers beauty
trembling mouths
tears trickle

death intercedes
lives that live
blood stained bodies
dance with sin

alone they stand
united they fall
the ones we slaughter
for no reason at all

DIM

dimmest of dim
ricochets gleaming skin
from this bag
under your eye
reflects our only sky
heaven's sweet kiss
evil venom's purge

evil venom's purge
the dimmest of dim
from your sweet stained face
to your blood-soaked flesh
through your internal maze
mesmerized by your cage

heated hell steals your feet
from the game you wish to keep
potent venom
seeps onto the soul
the soul you love
and wish to keep

THEN

you take my hand
i'll let you guide
me through the slaughter
we cannot heal
wipe my breast
when the walls crumble
covet my flesh

use your body
caress my soul
hold onto love
never let go

you take my hand
i'll let you guide me through the hurt
through the pain
take my body into yours
to happiness once again

take off my clothes
love what you see
tell me you love me
then…
set me free

6:00 IN THE MORNING

my love it's 6:00 in the morning
i am a mess
i haven't seen your face
i haven't heard your voice
i miss everything about you

i've been hanging on
my grip slowly slipping
my heart only aching
in this game of growth

i'm playing this game
trying not to call
crying when the voice on your machine
doesn't sound like you anymore

my love it's 6:15 in the morning
i am a mess
i haven't seen your face
i haven't heard your voice
i miss every little thing about you

CLOSE YOUR EYES

close your eyes baby
i'll kiss your sweet face
feel my lips
the pattern they trace
love too pure
close your eyes baby
feel what i feel

touch too tender
fight to resist
one touch with my wand
i could certainly miss
enveloped with passion
my body explodes
waves of emotion
unexplored roads

i hold your cheek inside my palm
my eyelids gently kiss
feel the power baby
it's what others miss

theatre in my mind
playing heaven all the time
now you are here
after endless grey skies
now you are here baby
thanks for dry eyes

fires of the past
i've doused the flames
unpack your bags baby
happiness remains

a surprising gift
grateful to receive
to see your face baby
is to re-believe
in all that i dreamt
that i prayed would come true
i feel in each moment
giving in to you

angels whispered promises
kept through years of pain
i knew there was you baby
holding me through the rain

tomorrow holds no promise
cast your fears aside
open your heart wider
savour this new ride

drink the love i pour you
taste the truth i prepare
only love exists
until infinity's there

SWEET LIPS

i see the sunlight
tighten strength
under darkness
stirring blank
in through glimmer
subtle wisps
upon my shoulders
i feel sweet lips

in the glory
between the grey
depths of weakness
eyes betray
in through shadow
spoken behind
upon my chest
i feel sweet lips

beyond your horizon
boundaries drift
melodious whispers
secrets shift
in through haze
blinding sin
upon my hand
i feel sweet skin

through my fingers
tracing flesh
across mother's breast
searching soul
in through pain
roaring waves
upon my cheek
i feel sweet lips

through my body
shivering spills
i grasp the flesh
feeling need
in through eyelids
squeezing close
upon my body
i feel sweet lips
my own

THE LONGING THAT KILLS ME

you are the light that wakes me
the darkness that scares me
the voice that soothes me
the sun that burns me

you are the thirst i quench
the hunger i feel
the taste i crave
the wine that takes me

the air i breathe
the wind that shakes me
the breeze that comforts me...
you are

you are the hand that loses me
the heat that melts me
the ice that freezes me
the beauty that captures me

you are the angel that guides me
the friend that helps me
the lover that amazes me
the Father that carries me

you are the whisper that intimidates me
the smile that lifts me
the happiness that feeds me
the sun that rains on me

the teardrops on my cheek
the sparkle in my eyes
the moisture on my lips
the cream between my thighs…
you are

you are the oil that softens me
the pinch that bruises me
the touch that steals me
the kiss that makes me cry

you are the strength that empowers me
the pain that transcends me
the joy that warms me
the will that changed me

you are the love that cleanses me
the hope that fuels me
the dream that drives me
the longing that kills me…
you are

FEATHERS

touched by gentle wings
the warmth of your feathers
dust my heart
tickle my flesh
your special presence
in sunshine's rays
on moonstruck nights
your wings caress my soul
i know you're home
your wings caress my heart
i know you are here again
your spirit transcends

peace cradles my head
the love of feathers
lift my smile
brush my wrist
your special presence
in glinting stars
on moonstruck nights
your wings envelop and swallow me
i am alive
i am free

your special presence in sunshine's rays
your special presence on moonstruck nights
your wings caress my entire soul
i know you are home
your wings caress my heart
i know you are here again

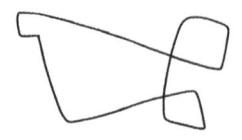

UPON YOUR SHOULDER

upon your shoulder
eyelids close
peace kisses
a tender soul
soothing sounds
sweet lips mend
a hurting heart

upon your shoulder
a brief escape
a grace of solitude
where trees caress
the harshest wounds
leaves swing promises of hope

upon your shoulders
water runs clear
a fountain of love
cleansing the raw sore
the warmest river of dreams
eyelids open

upon your shoulder
upon your shoulders
heaven on earth
or so it seems

BOUNDLESS

His grace was given
bore through love
each blessing seen
heard and felt
in mouths
boundless inspiration
generations of reciprocity
reciprocity
our hearts precious casings
boundless energy
energy given by His grace
in the heart sleeps the knowledge
in the heart keeps the soul
this energy deemed love
captivates
heals
protects
cures all

LIVE IN LIGHT

it's in my smile
that tilts its wave
hidden beneath
my fear love craves
to see your face
the sun and moon
whispering broken words
an unknown tune
i long for you
for you with me
through the long-dreaded night's eternity
'til the water halts
its shallow mist
and mother's children
remain unkissed
'til earth and shore
remain neutral tones
and wondrous worries
come to the known
'til sky and shark
embrace in sweet
'til ssshhh and song
simply retreat
until the deserts

deserted floor
knocks down forest's
secluded door
'til man and woman
charge in stride
'til black and white
hold hands with pride
until the darkness'
terrorizing gasp
fills up with love
light deserves at last
to be entwined with the arms i love
no darkness can keep me from
taking my place
i will be strong
the light i will chase
knowing in the end
light's shadow will be cast
upon your beautiful face
and only together
can we make dreams come true
so i will live in this darkness
'til i can live in light
with you

NOT THE GIRL

not the girl you used to be
not yet the girl you know
hearts beat in the wind
feel the breeze
look to the stars
i am where you are
nature is my friend
now i can be my best
in my sunset dress
slight burn on my chest
strumming strings
where's the music you want to write
where's your sunday dress
can you feel your thumb is already numb
can you play under the stars
where have you been
before the wind chimes song
a single note
smile
it won't be long
now is where you can be your best
sunday beautiful dress
tan on your chest
strumming strings

living my dreams
there is a sense
tufts of incense
you can rest
prettiest girl
you'll be your best

WHERE DO WE GO

always a question
where do we go
is there an answer
i do not know

a tunnel of light
they say it's pure beauty
brings on a fright
please where do we go

will we come back
from wherever we go
what is it like
this i don't know

are we safe to go down under
are we held through thunder
maybe i want to die
let the mystery out
do i want to die
the question is so
the answer of course
is
i don't know

ONE LOVE, ONE FEAR

succulent lips
heat transpires
voluptuous tasting
rapturous desire

a body too real
i love to touch
insecure i feel
i want it too much

a mouth just amazing
swallows me whole
the jaw devours
i have no control

paralyzed whirling
mind drifting and blank
a burst of tension
you're here now, who do i thank

my soul has left
you've sucked me in
my body is yours
is that such a sin

safety comes on strong
whenever you're near
just please don't hurt me
that's my only fear

I AM OKAY

i am okay
in black tar feet
and broken bones
of love
my eyes tired
my tears release
their strangling grip
suddenly they race
i am at peace

i am okay on rainy days
i am okay in sunshine's fade
i swallow the grey
that clutches my sweat
i live at peace
i feel no regret
i am okay

my eyes vision white
through dust-filled triumphs
of black and light
i live at peace
i am okay
i am okay
forever
today

FOR NOW

for now
i'm on the road
for now
i'm off to go
away with tears and frozen smiles
dimples escaping
each long while
for now

for now i'm free to breathe
the artist in me
a painting wizard
walls of love
no more hate
no more hate
the key that opened my heart
locked that crippling gate
no more hate
for now

for now i'm on the scale
weighing light as air
full of boundless energy
lots of love to spare
for now my heart is open
for now you were the key
thank you for each heartache
for now

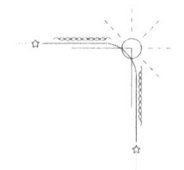

NEVER WANTED TO LEAVE

sometimes the day takes you
where you never intended
as the day turns to night
unaware of the questions

complicating your mind
strolling through misery
uncontrollable chatter
the intention is honour, somewhere

the pattern unruly
in the warp where you float
your minds eye is open
peace covets your soul

twirling winds escape my sweet hug
strong belt tightens around your gut
forces still looking for
what you once loved

will the shirt or the toke
make you believe or achieve
where will you be and who will you see
the day i drove i never wanted to leave

impossible questions wondering why
your shirt keeps me warm
the tokes take me high
where is the landing gear here in the sky

why is the breeze up here passing me by
that day i drove i never wanted to leave
the intention is honour, somewhere
that night i drove i never wanted to leave

HOMELESS

i bend to view
was that you
you walked by
walked by like you knew
do you know me?
do you know my life?
the way you walked
you turned your head
shot me a look
what do you think you know
i ask was that you
cause you looked like you knew
your attire
chasing aspire
your petty glance
your pretty face
says you know nothing
but you looked as if you knew
so i ask was that you
do you know what you looked at
cause it looked like you did
i am not one of you
you are not one of i
you think that i choose

but i'm forced to lose
i ask was that you
who knew someone big
who threw me out
is it disgust your little look was about
i disgust you
you disgust i
either way we are one
we do not choose to die
throw me spare change
spit in my face
you still have your life
i'm stuck in this place
i bend to view
i ask was that you
who gave me a glance
and looked like you knew
i laugh in your face
now go take your place
stand in your line
do what they say
i'm just here
pay me no mind
ignore the fact
that works in your world
either way
we're all here today
either way
we're all one
but i do not choose
i do not choose to lose
i do not choose to die

BACK TO ME

i cry myself to sleep
another sleepless night
wretched wrinkled worn
endless grey sky
i feel each tear from start to finish
softly bless my tired cheeks
i hope God can help
no one else i've found can
i wish for the love
in those innocent little voices
filling the park
full of joy and beauty
i wish to feel
more strongly
the moment you first carried me
through the long treacherous journey
back to me

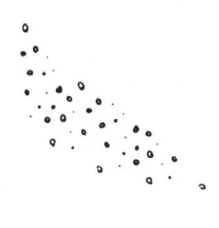

WHISPER

i feel
faintness
deftly caress
goosebumped flesh
inside
air sinks
forbidden depths
i feel
essence
subtle heat
beyond realms
swiftly retreat
i feel
solitude
sweetly spray
smiles spent
washed away
i feel
stillness
itching bones
i feel
your breath
though i
am alone

TEARLESS

i won't cry
the hollow inside
breathless whispers
your hand in mine

together we are
physically clung
miles apart
mindless drifts
but i won't tell

i won't cry
as inner pain persists
as if stitched
i'll remain silent
and i won't cry

gently as we move
passion stains the sheets
our bodies attract
penetration cuts deep
but i won't cry

hidden emotions
push to be heard
you are too deaf
i know but i won't say

i'll keep it to myself
without a tear
confined inside
this withering coffin

i understand you
But i won't show you
love is feared
hurt has occurred

selfish as it seems
i understand
i won't cry as you pass me by
but you have to promise
when my body speaks
you'll listen

when i stare blankly at the wall
please don't turn
don't ask what's wrong
because i might cry

please don't turn
don't ask what's wrong
i will cry
because i love you

JUST RIGHT

standing there in the country bar
in jeans, sparkly top, black coat
hadn't expected to go out that night
hadn't expected to be seen at all

standing at the wine barrel table alone
my friends hit the dance floor
i planned to go home
i danced at the table to watch our stuff
you strummed your guitar i noticed your scruff
and smiled

your lips as you sang in your red
plaid shirt
sweetly curled with each passing word
your eyes twinkled under the lights
your jeans hugged
your hips just right

i saw you come over to talk to our friend
i almost didn't hug you
i did in the end
your body was hard
you stood so tall
i told you
you're so sexy
that was all

you started your set from the table i watched
not only you
more closely
a crowded dance floor
which you clearly rocked

your lips as you sang in your red
plaid shirt
sweetly curled with each passing word
your eyes twinkled under the lights
i turned my gaze
your soul too bright
those dark black jeans
hugged your hips just right

when i saw your text light up my phone
i gave up planning
trying to go home
my lost smile found
in the sound of your voice
i gave in to my wine
danced all night
cause you said
stick around

your hot lips as you sang in your red
plaid shirt
sweetly curled with each passing word
your eyes twinkled under the lights
your jeans hugged your hips
just right

i knew you'd be fun
i still can't believe
i drove you home that snowy night
my life so wrong lately
yet you so right
i'm a city girl
i turned country that night

i kissed those sweet hot lips that sang
so nice
your red plaid shirt
out of sight
your hips perfectly free of those tight
black jeans
i lost myself
you found me

my life so wrong lately
yet you so right
i'm a city girl
i turned country that night

MOON

i've sat on this bench
a time or two
while wind and sun
comforted me
my thoughts would switch
their tunes
to hollow voices of solitude

it's in the wind i feel your touch
in the sun you keep me warm
it's in the wind i hear your silent whisper
still your moon remains untouched

i've paced this sand
a night or three
with cold sand kissing my toes
it's earth that heals me
nights like this
when God is the only one home

it's in the wind i feel your touch
in the sun you keep me warm
in the wind i hear your silent whisper
still the moon remains untouched

i've opened these arms
shed these tears
held my heart
torn my soul
all on a night or four
i've felt that wind
i've cooled the sun
even heard your little whisper...
but nothing is nothing
until something is something
and God doesn't answer your door
until fire is water
and earth meets shore
it's your moon that remains untouched
your beautiful moon
most precious moon
untouched

THAT'S THE THING ABOUT THE HEART: IT BREAKS

PART TWO

A LITTLE TEAR

a little tear
a little girl
as she grows
they disappear
kept inside
to be her secret
no one will know
or so she thinks
as she smiles to hide her pain
inside
holds many fears
that never disappear
when hurt again
they always reappear

LOST AT SEA

lost in a world
not even my own
the threshold holds nothing
i am unknown

looking outwards
nothing is there
field of empty dreams
i stand alone
bare

no help
from no one
better that way
i keep to myself
alone each day

my mind is full
so many things
nobody realizes
not everybody sings

blank with terror
my face is pale
my life is over
the ship couldn't sail

PIERCING

yearning for his touch
the petal of a rose
she misses so much
upon newly fallen snow

his delicate whisper
as a faint gust of wind
enters my heart
as a pin piercing skin

alone
the only tree in a forest
so hard to bear
a horse and a harness

a wish is all
i have like a dream
a fish out of water
is how it would seem

just a whisper or touch
all i ask
alone is how i feel
a dream all i have

ME

there i am to sit
bow in my hair
hands clasped
dimples dimpled
cheeks aglow

tears down my cheeks
hair stuck to my neck
never mind the frowned heart
tucked behind my breast

carry on as i should sit there
hiding scars that
bled for months
years
now scabbed over
under painted flesh

there i am to sit
neat and looking pretty
hair combed back
shirt tucked in
i don't think so
that's not me

SCORCH THE EARTH

i scorched the earth you stole from me
i scorched the dirt you threw in me
i scorched the church you gave false power
and i scorched your life inside my shadow
i scorched the hills
i scorched the sea
and scorch your life for scorching me
i scorched your smile inside my hate
i scorched you up
the sweet taste
i scorched my life
after tasting yours
and scorch you for giving me yours
i hate the given life
i hate eternal fate
i scorch the bed of roses
and tea you made
i scorch the water through sunshines fade
i scorch the trees and the grass
i scorch them all and it's no sin
'cause i've been scorched
and scorched by all
now, i scorch and rise, not fall
but i'd hate

to drink the blood
that floods your breast
and covets my faith
i'd hate to swim
in your river of death
and hate to be the rest
i hate the petty scream
i hate the life long dream
i scorched it up
when i scorched you
you scorch and won
i scorch and lose
and i hate that final thought
you scorch me
i forgive you not
you scorch and smile
i scorch and cry
who are you
to say live or die

ALL

all i couldn't give
all i couldn't say
leaves me blind
holy
every ordinary day

all i loved to see
all i loved to feel
is swollen up outside its
own
winding down its real

all i dreamt and hoped for
built up standing tall
silently crashed
feet wounded
destroyed them all

pain filled eyes
redness on my cheeks
wallowing misery
drowning me to sleep
haunted by
all the memories
i had once hoped to keep

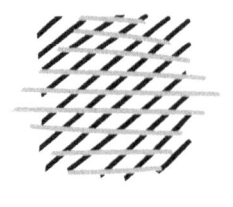

RAPIST

sacred sanctions
to be untouched
left alone
pondering

innocent eyes
disclosed by sweetness
rivers wandering
pried apart to flow

heart as gold
should never rot to waste
lips sneer and shiver
as burning tears start to race

bloodshed inside
functions appear to seize
unheard whispers
alive but never peace

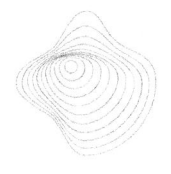

ALONE IN SILENCE

alone in silence
screams unheard
ready to explode
alone in silence
questions unheard
fluttering and scrambling
ready to burst
no one to answer
but that's not a first
alone in silence
explains her life
no words to describe
she could never say
why she sits alone in silence
day after day

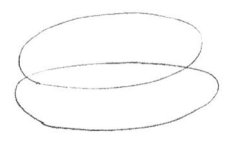

I DON'T WANT TO CRY TODAY

i don't want to cry today
when all that is torn is
damaged and bruised
bloodied and born
stolen and free
is when...
is when the smile of beauty rots
in its corruption seas
when the holy catches your fall
and graces your simple flee
is when my love...
only when my love..
your eyes will open to me

i don't want to cry today
in this blackened morn
and frosty eve that carries your scent
across the war
gently kissing my feet
i don't want to cry today

FEMININE

the world appears
in chaos
over a beautiful woman
forced to stay in her strong shell
it took many lifetimes to shave
unwelcoming
her positive vibes
the world is full of married men
who never know their wives
a beautiful woman in distress
longing just to be her best
without society's mess
estranged
she begins to move
love her only light
love her only breath
the world created for beauty
leaks heartache
suffocating the feminine
mother who births us all

HURTS TO CRY

i miss you
it hurts to cry
endless emptiness
hungry inside
feeding off the path of life
surprise after
surprise
yearning in my face
i miss you
it hurts to cry
goodbye i tried
goodbye i lied
i miss you
it hurts to cry
i miss you from
deep inside
a wound so sore
i covet your flesh
needless mistakes
never have i loved so much
i miss you
hurting
i cry

THERE IS NO ME

at times i long to hold you
there's nothing there
take you in my arms
show you i care

to walk along beside you
without you looking down
hold onto your hand
not scratching upon your ground

i'll have to let you go
end up where you'll be
i cannot stand beside you
myself i must set free

too many days i've stood
letting my mind tread
on one sided dreams
i never wanted to stop

i'll have to let you go
i've finally come to see
my visions are much clearer
inside, there is no me

GOD BETRAYED

inside beyond the depths
lie what God betrayed
solemn thoughts
possessing minds
tortured and distraught
externally unaware
silence is our plague
death is our fate
together further apart
outside we wait

HIT

hands unclench
poisoned insides
shelter from sin
hatred stained eyes

the stinging sensation
scarring flesh
verbal daggers
silently killing

prayers in the dark
ricochet off walls
emptiness echoes
scars never heal

smiles as sheets
presence to cover
damage to my innocent breast
bloodshot puffed
delicate eyes
full of hurt
tomorrow starts another day
to be hit again
while nobody knows

FALL

when you don't know anything at all
where is the space when buildings fall
silence that struggles to breathe through it all
no friend to call
will i be okay when mountains fall
will i be alone
or is there a place for me at the throne
one side of the darkness
change sets in
light is one focus
where to begin

I WALK

i walk the night with no one to protect me
solitude sweetens my bitter kiss
burns in a thousand dimensions
a thousand dimensions of pain

i walk the beach on quiet days
footprints indent the lonely soul
an autograph of betrayal
in a hundred dimensions that drain

i walk in my mind with you by my side
knowing you're somewhere else
you're thinking of her wishing i were she
should i be sorry i can only be me

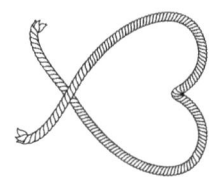

OPEN YOUR EYES

i wish when i looked
you would look too
open your eyes
look in front of you
see the light
encased within
search my soul
caress my skin
take my body
make us one
take what you see
what i have become
open your eyes
merge into mine
let her go
let us entwine
free your self
release the chain
binding you back
stale love once again
open your eyes
but do not attack
keep your head straight

no need to turn back
open your eyes
take a good look
what you could've had
she just took

IN TIME

under this almost-full moon
the eclipse, coming soon
i've left and loved
i loved and left
dying inside to begin again
scared as hell
the ties that bind
lengthy loops
wind inside
soul bursting through
nowhere left to hide
hitting walls
closing my eyes
spreading wings
cried all night
here on the floor
open my doors
singe my soul
wash darkness from light
hiding spaces
my internal fiery places
take my serious vibe
airy inside
let them see

situation is not me
let me see
eternal mirror
let light shine
let it be mine
in time

LEAKING LIES

one edge of the blade
leaning toward my face
thoughts of fear slap me
back into grace
i meditate
yet cannot replace
whispers leaking lies
against fate
internal hate meets
the holy gates
twists of truth pierce
old pains
inside again
inside a grain

THE GAME

as this deal tweaks
cards bending steel
untethered soul
divide
visions collide
inside dreams
visions die
wild death
hope up in flames
desertion
blame
blind

GLIMPSES

there's a place for you
i'll hold space for you
i see your heart
i feel need
illusion we bleed
who is happy anyway
believe in dreams
all fantasy
stories told
an endless stream
believe the dream
what do we believe
how do we conceive
notions magic potions
art or poetry
write in the night
riding the light
glimpses …sparkles
shards of glitter
mind a flitter

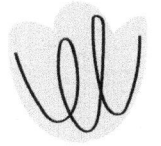

ALIVE IN THE GLITCH

out of the shape of our lives
destiny's journey retrieving the hide
shadowed silhouettes saddened inside
pressure in pounds of honour and pride

longing in frequencies
distant cries to transcend
screams greet beginnings
sirens kiss the ends
alive in the glitch
swimming to bend

BACKYARD BREEZE

here she sits
this pretty girl
full of hope in a backyard breeze
and dreams
tears pierce her eyes
no surprise
pretty girl
shattering nightmares
crying never ends
fear and doubt
no way out
tears and pain
leading you here
writing again
passion
dreams
go ahead little darling
see new angles
stand on your feet
let the tears fall in the backyard breeze

MICHAEL STONE

crying for months
attached
sad
because i'm attached
tears still flow
how long was i asleep
i don't care to know
buried in life
by beautiful snow
'til we met
awake in the world
you said its ok
to take an extra breath
my heart felt the words
my body felt joy
i took an extra breath
never the same without you
you've lit the way
sparked my sparks
travelled the world
cleaned up the parks
now who will it be
that shows me the way
teaches me to live

to awaken
hurts that you're gone
my practice lives on
can't say goodbye
crying for months
i bow deeply
risen in love

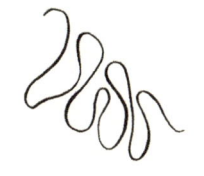

LOST IN LOVE

smoking and writing
in the dead of the night
eyes swollen from tears
heart shining bright

show me the light
through my burning gaze
lead me to joy
through this new pain

have i fallen in love again
hopeless at heart
hopeless at love
what does it mean
if none of the above

lost in love
with my life anew
lost in a sea of feelings
i have towards you

STOLEN

i wonder where you are
my silent screams of fear
piercing and forceful
lost amidst my ocean of life
adrift on horizons of fear
a haunting equation
wish you were here

i sit here feeling
down the darkest hole
dirt covers my face
no glimpse of light
tragedy unseen
external inside
full with infinite fear

i'm tired as i fight to surrender
lose my place as a rock
it breaks all spirit
force of the flow
pushes us out

broken wing
energy shift
temptations game
for the keen broken girl
cries for a lift
alone in fear
thoughts steal her gift

ILLUSION

hush of confusion
blindness plagues the earth
solid ground without a path
caught in impermanence
corpse of endless desires
where to turn
no place to run
journeys await discovery
destination a mere
illusion

DAMAGE DONE

one day you'll be sorry
the nasty things you say
fear drives you
committed to love for life
abusive words you choose to say
i cannot
will not stay
one day you'll be sorry
where you lay your fears
hate and anger
it's not for me to say
not my path to stay
i'll honour my peace and
believe again
undoing the damage
you've done
with love

NIKO

loving you
feeling you in places
i've never felt before
hear your voice
feel your soul
filling voids i've never known
without you
before you
wanting to be near you
listening
smelling
touching
your endless skin
loving you

tears from my heart
warmly bless my cheeks
loving you angel
from my universe of the deep
wish you were here
beside me
skin to skin
could we begin again

never change a moment
loved you through them all
angels near us
angels heal us
love you baby
love you angel
loving you has been it all

love mommy

FIREBALLS

the hits keep on coming
curveballs
fireballs
every hour today
first this
second that
third fourth fifth and sixth
lucky seven
i see your game
to inflict pain
to stir my pot
fill me with rot
sad you don't know peace
sad you won't go with grace
trying to steal mine
more wasted time
a dead end line
milking my fine
strengthening
my peace of mind

BLESSINGS OR BEGINNINGS

losing it
losing it all
leaving it there
wherever or whatever it is
drowns these tears
makes me incomplete
take it
take it all
i'm an empty vessel
trucking through hell

no words in my mind
tears
warm and streaming
blessings or beginnings

STAYING ASLEEP

when the winds are up
don't know what to say
it's easiest to close your eyes
passing your life away
into the halls of wasted love
disguised as genuine
splattered walls of life
that i called mine
watch it fade into memory's gaze
you missed the dancing angels in the light

CHOICE

wanting to live
caught in a scream
a fairy's dream
confused
what i have seen
what is real
choose not to tangle
with in-betweens
i'll give you what you are

waiting for a glimpse
a taste no more
more strength in me
than your fear
of accepting dreams

SEAMS

forever never seems long enough
for where you are
in the flowing love rivers of tomorrow

forever never seems long enough
for us to be a silent sea
an ocean's depth

forever never seems long enough
between us
promise me forever please
i beg you like innocence
on the crown of my knees
pleading
hoping on the promise
of years and years

forever never feels long enough
for the love river deep as the ocean
fresh as the sea
flowing between you and me

forever never seems long enough
the thought of losing you
leaves me breathless
in a sea of tears
no raft afloat
my eyes close
promise me forever more
forever never seems long enough

YEARNING

alone
alone
dressed up inside
nowhere to go
no one to see
an open world
a vast sea

alone
alone
waves crash harder
spirit soars higher

alone
alone
all dressed up inside
nowhere to go
like everyone knows

alone
alone
lonely like a bright light
hearts far away
inner demons shout
i'm astray
bring me to my companion
this life end
oh end this strife

ALL THE DRAMA

before all the drama
eyes locked from afar
liked what we saw
made our own choices
trusted what
we didn't know

before all the drama
free with each other
walked endless streets
drank in the music
laughed 'til we cried
nothing to hide

before all the drama
for two years we were free
liked what we saw
liked what we could be
finding the first peace
in our smiles, hearts, our touch

before all the drama
it was magical kisses
healing our hearts
before all the drama
you and me
in those days we were free

DENIED

idiotic moments
i felt you in mine
wishes fallen
holding hands
i tried
pleaded
you denied me
your presence
your time
no room by your side
changing tide
thoughts have lied
my pride has died
another by your side
you'll be fine
my efforts, words, gestures
denied
another girl awaits
a familiar pain
a life long train
stinging cheeks
i can barely see
so blind
believing

in our time
blindsided
hindsight
blinding
denied

AGAIN

i'll unplug the lights
remove the silly nightgown
again

i'll sit and watch
the fire turn to amber
not knowing
how you feel
i hoped you'd show up
again

nothing seems real
let the cat come up
kiss my boys g'night
again

the light in me begins to fade
flames of the fire turn to shade
one more sip in this thin wine glass
another day spent alone without you
again

what can i say
do i beg you
why
insecure lies
over too many days
again

up to you i said
you never came
not a word
in this game
i don't feel the same
more hurt than anything
again

SECOND

you sleep with her
you told me
insecurity grips me
feeding me lies
i'm beside you yet
she's who you want

we sleep side by side
if she was me
would you hold me
would you open your eyes
look my way
and smile
if she was me

it tugs my soul
you can't let her go
we're so different
i've no security
no control

you sleep with her
you told me
it's all i think about
my creative vibes lost
insecurity grips me
makes me feel old
it tugs my soul
you can't let her go

no matter what i say
no matter what i do
the million tiny things
that show i love you
don't matter any more
your heart is somewhere else
you'll never love me back
in love with someone else

you sleep with her
you told me
insecurity's in control
it's what i think about
in your arms
on your chest
second best

whispering i love you
thinking you won't hear
fearing you won't stay
i'm not enough for you
she has what i don't
she has you

before i could lie to myself
before you ruined my day
i pushed uncertainty away
now it's in my face
it's every place
the words replay in my mind
wishing we were fine

wish i made you feel so good
wish you'd always want more
wish i could make you crave me
wish you'd stick to my soul
wish she didn't have a hold on you taking you away
wish i had magic tricks
a genie
a magic wand
wish we'd stay us
wish i was your one

you sleep with her
you told me
it's all i think about

NOT WITH ME

you're not where i want to be
you're not the chorus that sings through me
i want divine
your attention in mine
love
hearing feeling real
in my eyes
between my thighs
lots to realize

you never told me anything
never how you felt
i guessed
wrong
your actions
wrong
no boundaries to admire
a sneaking feeling always
hiding
not desire

you could never be with me
always with your phone
always something to hide
i cannot be
where you're not with me
i want a partner in crime
you're not where i want to be
i'll see you
in time

DREAMING SOUL

wanted to be what i thought was free
to believe but it wasn't me
to sail the highest towers
swim the tallest shores
feeling and breathing
a lifetime kiss of wonder

wanted to be what i thought was free
to slay the enemy of my dream
to log the deepest entries
climb the grandest trees
an angel swinging solo
dancing in the breeze

wanted to be what i thought was free
to deny I was the girl i'd seen
to live the greatest story
sing in love at ease
an angel feeling breathing
a lifetime on her knees

UNDERTOW

one last tear before i go
into a world long known
high society within
breeding culture alive in sin

one last tear before i go
a prayer to take you there
caste is slowly fading
candor false decor

one last tear before i go
smile twisted frown
desirous lips
last glimpse of light

one last tear before i go
one last tear

CHARRED INNOCENCE

watching the burn
charred innocence

galleys remain calm
distance sweet

watching the burn
your essence strong

charred innocence
slowly withdrawn

you felt the tears
watching them burn

my charred innocence
never return

CURIOUS

satin lace padded
confined inside
lies one girl's innocence
and one mans pride

a beaten beauty
once trembled in peace
to one a daughter
to the murderer a niece

fake portraits of joy
the sleek mellow tone
she smiled to keep
her horror unknown

love was sought
forever out of reach
her quest to escape
while his to teach

worthless words
pinning her down
unheard motions
another ripped gown

silence prevailed
in a house she wished knew
the blood from her veins
she left as their clue

VORTEX

you know i have sat in darkness
shaded through the vortex
of a mind split in pieces
through the valley's rotten thesis
you know i have lived a thousand years
in a mannequin mold of melted wax
feeling black on my shoulders
through the rivers burned
you know i have tunnelled racist slurs
escaping life too sick to purge
torn and twisted held intact by the vortex

you know i have stripped the camouflage
that tears blood from the eyes
through the mountains hidden caves
stark red wrinkles of the age
you know i have creamed the naked beast
shadowed by the vortex

peeling life stained fingers off corroding corpses
you know i've wept right where you crack
transcending hymns to swim golden miles
i lie awake out of tomb
i am still in darkness blinded
by piercing silhouettes in the vortex

RUINED

eyes gaze hopeless
across the shimmer
squinting for answers
slice or let me be

walking the distance
the mind cannot see
endless footpaths
the blade is still

as i reach you penetrate
again i'm forced to be yours

the grasp is strong
you made the move
i made my mark
piercing the flesh you already had

as i take my life now
you're to blame
for i already died then

LINKED

sinfully immortal
i stand alone
solitude confines
as chains develop inside
the tissues of love
fragmented forever
exploited and open
left dangerously raw

sinfully immortal
my hands caress
the flesh of visions
i engage to impress
nakedness so sweet
abandoning my thoughts
i strive for the soul
as my mind warns
i fear not

blades as nails
tearing open the flesh
blood floods in warning

cutting deeper
i slice beyond the unknown
territory forbidden
sinfully exposed

trespasser's beware
flesh covets our souls
but the scars
we all share

I LIE

i lie awake
amidst the rain
intellectually blind
as if i am
in someone else's room
i lie awake
amidst the snow
unconsciously forbidden
i lie awake
though perhaps i shouldn't
i fell beyond
into the depths
clothed from what i knew
i fell beyond
into the depths
and lie awake nude
i lie awake
amidst the hail
constructed in the mind
censoring thoughts
seemingly behind
peacefully alone
i lie awake

sheltered by the flesh
of someone's mistake
alone
in pain
i lie

SISTAR

often thinking
of words unsaid
feelings hidden
beyond in depths
without a trace
withering alone
inside each vein
wondering when
time will come
to meet the chance
to speak
to reveal
hidden trenches
of feelings
flooding
silence preyed
tearing apart
emotions felt
in most
my heart
today
miles separate
physically
older sister

loved
protected
cared for
in thought
everyday
while silent
patiently awaiting
a day to scream
now sitting
ticking time
time has come
as i cry
feeling alone
tears possess regret
all the things
i should have said
never did
my only sister
i love you

MISSING YOU

have i forgotten to tell you something
as i sit in this hotel room
twenty-five floors from you and i
i sense there is something more to say

i wonder...

did i kiss you goodnight long enough
have i sent enough prayers
babe you mean the world to me
all my love is there

inside i feel you whisper
cause i cannot seem to close my eyes
i wonder what you are doing
as i sit here so far away
with thoughts of you i cannot escape

i wonder...
did i kiss you goodnight long enough
have i sent enough prayers
can you feel you are the world to me
all my love is there

baby take what you can handle
the rest i'll keep alive
inside my heart that burns for you
on each wave that i must ride

tell me tomorrow baby
have i missed something for you
is there more i need to send
as i sit so far away

have i sent you goodnight kisses
have i sent enough sweet prayers
know you are the world to me
baby, all my love is there

close your eyes my prince
feel my lips upon your forehead
sleep tonight in peace little angel
tell me tomorrow you're okay

IT'S IN EACH TEAR

i know sometimes
it's hard to play
with things that often change
it's hard to be consistent
yet, playing with love
is a dangerous game
i know that my tears
will make no change
yet, its all my heart can say
with each tear
draping my softened flesh
is a hope that things will change
although you could never know
it's in each tear draping my flesh
my screams of pain are bleeding
in each tear my heart is broken and needing
it's in each tear
ripping apart my mind
it's self and inner beauty
my body longs to find

HAUNTED

the tainted mirror reflection
multiple faces distort reality
wasted white confiscated by red
the image haunts
portrait of death

liquid fills to rims of happy
one shut will ruin its beauty
gliding deeper spoiling sweetness
the tear widens
the melts ice

beyond the colour beyond the black
atop the circles between the lash
suspended in satanic time
screeching voices tune subtle rage
the image alive
portrait of life
portrait of death
the image haunts
the haunting image
haunts

ROHYPNOL

dressed up nice
big night tonight
year one class reunites to dance
stealing glances out the door

smiles wide the world is yours
reading writing fulfilling dreams
statue of strength will to succeed

heightened glory light and love
friendship dances
three-way hugs
life before a drink or drug

smiles wide the world is yours
reading writing fulfilling dreams
statue of strength will to succeed

slowly turn around
creepy predator a stolen crown
false smiles dirty dreams
infected drink muffles your screams

smiles hide the world outdoors
animals attacking the angel's dreams
fallen statue no glory to succeed
free will of man leaves the angel to bleed

SIT ALONE

when i've caught the day
inside my hands
blew it kisses
far and wide
held the angel's
birthday wish
touched the fragile
breaking wisp

when i've melted in vain
sweet melody
poisoned valley's eternity

when i've kissed my last
bitter kiss
wished my last
holy wish
felt the residue
softly fade
sat beyond the tree's pink shade
held the hand
of frigid cold
blessed the young
from which comes old

when i've ran the last mile jump
smelt the last array of dump
tasted its sweet meringue
swallowed its bitter tang

when i've welded holy grass
to mountain tops of tarnished glass
left the burn to sweetly rage
upon the palace's tinted cage

when i've kissed my last sweet kiss
is when the day you'll truly miss
you sit alone to wait your turn
i'll spark that final burn
you sit alone watching TV
tell yourself it was always me
you sit alone
you sit alone
i cannot wait
'til you sit alone

TEARS

there is peace in the coolness
of the air that caresses
my skin tonight

the stars are in the sky
the leaves are blowing in the breeze

distant sounds of the highway
fading in and out
as cars and wind
fill the peace in this night

my eyes are swollen and red
i've cried for hours today
depth of the ocean
into my soul
your words have cut me open

my wounds been exposed
the chill that keeps me company
is all that i can know

smoke escapes my lips
ties that i have bound
i've felt this pain before
and underneath i'm found

my son hears me cry
my friends listen
are these tears from
the depths of my own hell

RIVER

rivers of emptiness
tears gently flow
up roaring inside
each tear holds a wish

a wish for forgiveness
and many more
a smile at least
what could that hurt

hurt is constant
as the river flows
a streaming pain
that nobody knows

confined inside
drowning she sinks
the rivers are rapid
sanity washes away

swamps of emptiness
fear hurt desolation
up roaring inside
as tears spill below

she waits alone in solitude
waiting for the wave
to splash her face
and wash the pain away

YOU BURN

with every breath
with every word
too much unsaid
too much unheard
silently penetrating
desperate thoughts
your voice
is lost
with emptiness sought
in each attempt
a secret burn
violation
only to return
returning to depths
beyond visions realm
silently you burn
scorching out of control
purpose's virtue
you have no gain
secrets slither slowly
bitterness remains
hung by choice
silently you burn
in a life of emptiness

with no return
too much unsaid
too much unheard
with every breath and every word
all you do is burn and burn

RAPE IS THE NAME

smiles of youth just fun to be had
darkness descends nothing to fear
loss of feeling with every step
feet reaching the ground
nothing to suspect

hunters swarm their prey
the innocent walk unaware
blinded by liquid poisoned in veins
bloodshot eyes the obvious clue

eyes lift smiles exchange
darkness descends her eyes must close
to her a friend
letting herself go in trust

to him an opportunity
knocking the door
of a twisted mind
advantage taken while beauty sleeps

unconscious meets conscious
visions clear
flashbacks frightening
nothing to fear

reality slaps hard
smiles fade to shame
even though a friend
rape is still the name

FIST OF HATE

on pleasant earth
baby's breath unheard
soul contemplates heaven
the mind reminds
death death death
a step until the axis winds
death more positively inclined
selfish greed
possessing veins
truth betrayed
contrasting view
white captures blue
a fist of hate i never knew
contaminated blood
frying flesh
death death death
no turning back
a black silhouette
and baby's breath
never heard

HARDEST PART

i sit
broken hearted
bleeding for freedom
screaming apart

loving myself
the hardest part

ANGEL EYES

i look in my mind
to see what is in yours
who do you think of
when you break through each door
where is the honour
you shoot to subside
how does the danger
chill you inside

fake where you run
tear away those you hide
chase the dragon on the other side
deepen the trance of naked extremes
catch your wizard
steal your dreams
angel eyes guide you astray
angel eyes on your soul each day

RISE OF THE GODDESS

PART THREE

I COULD

if i had to live without your eyes
your face
your touch
if i had to live without loving you so much
if i had to close my heart
so full of you
i could

i could
imagine a life without your smile
your body
your skin
if I had a life so indescribable
if i had to live without you
terribly weak
could you?

if i had to live without you
i could
since every time my eyelids kiss
i feel your body's length
i lay atop your chest
your hand warm across my lower back
so full of you
i could

i could
because i hear your breath
i feel you breathe
from all the nights we lay so close
i feel my fingers caress your skin
i fall more heavenly in love with you
again just by the thought
if i had to live without you
i could

i could because i have been without
you every day for years
but the times we are together
i keep alive when we're apart
i have each word
each touch
each smile
each kiss
held safely in my heart

i could
live without you
hold every memory
but i'd rather live peacefully with you
each minute precious time together
new memories new stories
fresh laughs fresh tears
i dream
i could

i could laugh with you
forever
i could hold you
forever
touch you
smell you
see you
accept you
cherish you,
be thankful for you
grateful for you
bless you
love you
from the home within my heart
where God is universal
where you are
forever
i could

OCEAN OF PEACE

in an ocean of peace
hearts sail to the depths
of broken wings
through silent stings
inches of earth
distraught in touch

in an ocean of peace
guidance release
afloat the flurry
rampant winds
inside the healing
thrusts to begin

in oceans of peace
where is the space
that longs for breath
the treasurer's grace
drifting abroad in tides
through storms
i felt the love
that needs no more

an ocean of peace
wraps its wings
keeping the heart afloat
an ocean of peace
captures the breath
losing every thorn
an ocean of peace
steals the sail
until the endless sky
wraps its wings into my soul
forcing me to fly

an ocean of peace
God's loving embrace
only just a taste
to wet the dust
and hold you to your feet

an ocean of peace
the sweetest place
to rest your tired limbs
bathe in beauty found within
there is no other place
an ocean of peace
to soak your toes
cleanse your worried fear
an ocean of peace
close your eyes
feel

DREAM

in the hollow of the dream
feel the relentless scream
dying to the end you've already seen
in thought
in prayer
the world has left you
naked
bare

in the hollow of the dream
you wish and scream
to an audience
out of sight
someone appearing black as night
as you wish
you close
naked
and bare

you dream the hollow dream
though no one's there
alone in the silent
still of the fright
you repeat your episode

night after night
with thought and prayer
since no one is there

in the hollow of the dream
you twist and scream
unaware
bare
nothing as it seems
you tear a wet stream

in the hollow of your dream
you could not see
you're wrapped in warmth
of piercing wings
naked and raw
you create this stream
a world of blessing
you've yet to dream

ONE LOVE

i met a man who loves like me
i crossed the world
i swam the seas
believe in angels
believe in dreams
nothing is what it seems
love is everything
destiny
brightest stars in a darkened sky
love travellers of the universe
angelic messengers
you and i

WE

reflections beautify this year
with, of, beside, beneath
you
happy seeds of love
dancing ribbons vibrate within
minds wide open
gorgeous fires burn
heart and soul alive
beautiful music, who you are
gratitude fills our path thus far
we are humble
we are kind
we inspire others
we hunger and we thirst
we seek and we acquire
we have fun together
beautiful beacons
lessons learned
beautiful dance
of who we are

I AM THAT FORCE

i am the heroine in your movies
tainted in your veins
angel in your dreams
planner of elaborate escapes
height of extremes
bearer of visions
practiser of known
smiles on their faces
light behind frowns
castle and underground
present every birth
feeling every drown
owner of the dunce
owner of the crown
i am that force moving around

TRUST

know your strengths
weaknesses
friends
love your enemies
yourself
trust yourself
keep it simple
avoid excesses
in body and mind
believe
dream
stay strong
persevere
live in the moment
surrender
never give up
ignore drugs
honour temptation
listen
feel
be thankful
be humble
write
laugh

sing
dance
take a chance
be fearless
reassess
forgive
move forward
love

IF YOU FORGET

if you forget
when winds are high
blowing thoughts of separation
through your mind
remember
those are only fears
pull out a tool
a spiritual practice
i'll reflect light back to you
because you chose me that night
you were the light in my darkness
i'll be the light in yours
if you forget you're a star
i'll remind you
you are
not your past
not your mistakes
not what you think you are
you are
perfect

TRUST WE MUST

release the chains
that bind
our self-created living hell
vision jewels and tools
within you
dig deeper
you are the creator
of your experience
your life
forgiveness comes
knowing we are blind
we write the ending
we must
believe in ourselves now
we must

BODHICITTA

there you are
never far
always here for me
reasons i've yet to see
listening
absorbing limits i cannot see
free as i seem
a teacher searching
learning
the toughest lessons to begin
a life was born
i'm convinced in sin
where to begin
bodhicitta within
the bud of a lotus
an ocean
leans on the shore
having it all
full
wanting craving more
depths of the soul
i explore

NIGHT OF CANDLELIGHT

night of candlelight
passions of my soul
basking hot wonders
aloneness a oneness
in control
flame of intention
sparking desire
surge to the tips
of my burning wants
douse the oils
soothing taunts
extinguish excess
beyond eternal flames
extreme healing today
burning away
into the light
night of candlelight

SURRENDER

to live in each moment and feel love
no greater joy exists
we all have a dream
come so far travel so deep
unveil who we are
grace and beauty no longer myths
love and peace the only bliss
the planet exists in the change of your thoughts
succumb
to what's real
extinguish
fires that scar
ignite love and passion
breathe and just be
no weight upon your soul
only thought
surrender fear
savour breath
with love

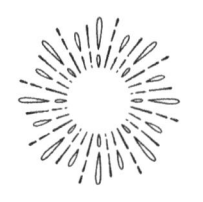

SHINE

times so long standing apart
away from the ache
stress on the heart
hero beyond words
in a fellow's world
beyond real
mystical mountain
uninformed soul
desert rose buried
itch for grace burn for love

depths of darkness
forbidden desires
arising from ashes
fuel for more fires
feed your blaze
ignite your fire
feed your power
fuel your knowledge
know your thirst
quench your dreams

PURPOSE

i feel a thrush
a sudden rush
pull to open
to find me again
release a full cup
a wandering mind
fighting alive
chasing thoughts
escaping dreams
living in a natural scene
beginning to believe again
write from space
to land in a place
of purity

OMNIPRESENCE

sweetest lullaby
sun kissed sky
beholding the breast of movement
swallowing solitude
moisturizing organs
peace is a smile we feel

my soul dances
holds my breasts
raptures thee

one heart one love
below and above
breathtaking omni
gasping with love

AWAKE

passing sense
gifts of transience
juices of berries
scents of fairies

happiness sprouts
petals of rain
drops of delicious
tastes of sunlight
kisses of fate

kiss's comprehension
movement entwined
spirals of believing
twisting
spinning
freedom

colour flashes
symbol dances
eyes a flutter
love forever

RAINBOWS

silk shiny silhouette
tasty liquid velveteen
heavenly dainty pet
worlds to meet you yet

circles of light
envisions of you
deliciously beautiful
deliciously you

coloured skies of grace
wondrous rainbows of mystery
prisms are my eyes
opening unfolding
honest and true
colours of you

WALKING THE PATH

i am a strong heart
beating with strength
gathered in arms
from trenches i've sank
i am a strong heart
beating bandages with beauty
baby steps to freedom
i am a strong heart
walking forward gripping faith
marching forward to my fate
closing each new gate
i am a strong heart
no matter what you hate
my love a tornado
strong hearts never shake
i am a strong heart
love 'til i break

THE KEY

memories of a broken heart
deserted
chapters in the dark
brought to the light
from newer times of darkness
a chance to feel
chance to heal
the years passed
no lapse
where hearts have been touched
there exists no patch
where there once was love
there can be no rehash
just a chance to heal
a chance to love better than before
love never dies
i am sure it hides
the key's inside the mind

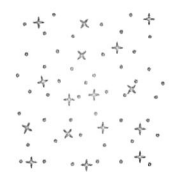

THE MOUNTAINS

the better you look
the less the others will tell you
it's nothing you'd find on a poster or book
it's the life you choose
that God's placed on your path
a balancing act
you've already won
the strongest soldiers
still battling with fear
lay your thoughts to rest
the end is clear
light abolishes darkness
sustained through eternity
there is light within each eye
seek and enjoy each shine
its nothing you'd find on a poster or book
it's wisdom beyond what the others mistook

CREATION

touching the tip of the gift
lost in twist and find
sand dunes love land mines
journeys kiss tides
breath of the alive
tasting sweet skin within
jolting thoughts
to whose chagrin
melting the mold
creating the platter
world's colliding cosmos and matter
air earth reunion
fire water fusion
dances of energy in you and me

YOU'RE THE ONE

a brief interlude of space
the matrix holds you
fight to escape
as a child you wince
cinching delicate lids
hope for a dream
to blanket the flames
that torch your sweet skull
fight to escape
can't let you go

your curious eyes stretch
open in desperation
the light will blind
your tired heart
heal with warmth
your crescent flesh
veins will fill with light
your smile will rule the sun

glide through crashing waves
they come as practice
you be the rock
God has sent you
oceans of fear
crash at your feet
slipping away in tears

love
your blood
rules your guise
float through life
wings of wisdom
you've earned beyond the tears
you've earned beyond the years

NEW PATTERNS

exhale of relief
your footprints in the sand
i could have been in your arms
the whole time
smile in awe
elation so sweet
inviting
a higher ride
release the fear
fly through my open heart
feel what was already there

ONE CANDLE

sitting in smoke through the flames
one candle lit for hope
one for pain
i'm going to feel this pain again
i'm going to feel love transcend

i may be down for hours
i may be down for days
but something that doesn't
drown me down
will float me up again
i'll reach that silver lining
the last note i will touch
i've died a thousand deaths
yet i've dreamed as much

YOGA

my dear
i am the girl loving hard
how you see me struggle
i'll do the same for you
in time visions set clear
i will love you just as hard
my dear

my gift is aching
channelling pain and tears
inside your soul
my dear
my gift gives you back control

i am the weakness strength has charred
sensitive silhouette dancing afar
i'll do the same for you
in time dreams set clear
i will love you just as long
my dear

my gifted sense
channelling aches and fears
inside your soul
my dear
my gift gives you back control

two times
strike hard
dreams depart
down the aisle
bristles tickle our hearts
standing tall
strength to fall
fighting currents grasping walls
illusion unclear
my love washed in fear

i am calm
i'm the reward
i'll teach the same to you
in time
my dear

my gift is teaching
opening channels of love
touching you
lighting you
inside your soul
giving you back control

my love
my dear

ALIVE

to breathe feel
taste and swallow
temptation
from thy satin lips
my gates have widened to
compromise
angel's wings and heaven's scent
i am alive
no fear or regret
from burning bridges
crashing dreams
the light
bursting through
seams of intelligence
logic
i rock the boat that covets my smiles
tightens my throat
i am alive
to taste each breath
i am alive
without contest
upon the soil of deserted years
i open my heart

drown my fears
love is alive
i feel each breath
the opposing force
i have already met

TRANSFORMATION

a rebirth as we're brought together
you see the scars
looking at yourself
once hurt so bad
now just a scar
no pain
chains release your neck limbs and back
freedom letting go
like dropping down a waterslide into a pool
of darkness
rebirth
begins healing and rest
eyes soar as new once more
one last plug
to pull from your soul soon
confused and questioning
as a little child
so the teacher does teach
new friends by your side
what is real
you know because you feel
the world is fear
the cross at the road is finally here
rebirth

makes sense what you hear
truth
you fight not to believe
so sick and weak
you cannot go back
makes sense what you hear
you've always known
rest now for training and rebirth
show me your strength
i beg you
the technique is not your weakness
still you want to think
take your time
you don't succeed
open the door
it's time
to free your mind
fear doubt and disbelief
paralyzing grip
take the jump onto the stones
you'll rise again
a little sore you'll bleed
more rest
answers are coming
i glide by your side
know i believe
lessons taught
tempt your quest
beware fresh prince
nothing at once
fear is muted
when love is present
practice the fuel
ignite your fires
fear will tempt your power
ignorance is never bliss
the oracle awaits
you'll hear what you need
follow your path to you
a rebirth

know thyself
as you know love
walk your first steps
start to believe
you can see clearly
you know what to do
the means is provided
use your power
walk through your fears
together we rise above
complete the circle
you'll notice me when
i slip from view
we have saved each other
through and through
the difference between
knowing and walking
you now see
more battles will come you cannot foresee
fear will tempt you seriously
you're on your own
fears soon overthrown
after beating and running
you play in the game
you know it's not real
i wait by your side
encouraged by belief
you will one day
not feel a thing
just when you think
fear has won
and your heart stops
one kiss from love
is enough
to ignite your soul
to feel and know
belief and love
rebirth
take a deep breath
you'll never be the same

NEW MORNING

new days
fresh dawn breaking waves
escalate deliverance
golden horseshoe eclipse
beginnings birth
eyes wide envision
practice keeps the fragile forgiven

dreams shine through
pinholes of reality
cascade the force of light
eliminate untruth and darkness
the illuminated mind
is silent

INNOCENCE

inhale
see your face in the trees
let go
shiver
enjoying the breeze
deep breath
eyes wide
creating movement inside
taste of wind
brings wellness within
slight glances recognize
at the start line again
a return to innocence

HEALED

smallest glance and years are healed
nature of love
words strung together
crashes of words
deep inside
reflections of a crescent
moon outside
memories of satellites
inside sparks of fire
yearning
burning
lights twinkle
love more
seeing is movement
entertainment of the heart

SOUL OF A GIRL

strength in the soul of a little girl
lost and found
journey never ceasing
spirals of romance
catching sweet toes
love within hearts
all we can know
what's real is not the length
how deep
illusions veil
blindness is dirty
love never fails

TRUST THE PROCESS

openings need space
writing is grace
wrapped in love
vessels to the taste
no sin can win
in a warm embrace
passion shared
sparks flared
no sin can win
you're a beautiful space

TRIPPED ON A JEWEL

i've dreamt a million dreams
so it seems
i've travelled a trillion roads
tripped on a jewel or two
i've held onto love in my hands
kept all of my dreams alive
inside
here i am under my veil
writing to exhale
here i am in the prettiest dress
my heart is with you
wherever you are
i have been living for this day
for the moment
to look into your eyes
making promises come true

BREATHING

breath can hold anxiety
breath can hold my fear
breath has been carrying me through the years
as the river flows
so has... my life
have i breathed life into its beauty
have i polluted its stream
where will i be
where have i been
who
always...
who

JIU JITSU

little fighter
i get back up
jiu jitsu to teach you
a candle to your strength
internal grace
peace
freedom
joy
heart
soul
universal soul healed at last
close the gap
lost to found
sand to solid
strength of ground
jiu jitsu to teach you
i can see what you do
look for light
light you see

ONE MORE

many a day you try to fool me
i know you're there
i feel you in each tear
i feel you as you kiss them away
i know it's you
who turns my thoughts to God
all i want to do is think of you
you take them from me
because you know how much i hurt for you
you know how much i love you
i feel you love me more
that's why you help me up when i tremble
bless me when i break
but it's hard to breathe and smiles hurt
because i can't share them with you
i miss your face
do you miss mine
nothing i wouldn't give
to see you one more time
one more hug
one more smell
one more touch
one more smile
a million more i love you's

i cannot let you go
when i try i fall
you were the feet that carried me
the body that moved me
the strength that gave me life
without you i'm weightless
empty as time and unloved as earth
the mornings i get up
i know you pushed me
the nights i sleep
i know you hold me and keep me in your arms
some days my eyes are hot with hurt
empty sockets where you were
my shoulders cold
a shiver freezes my heart
a broken organ waiting
waiting for your warmth
yearning a painful yawn
how you used to heal me
your magical essence
mending broken hearts
disappearing tears and smiles
entwined entangled arms
how you used to heal me
soothe my soul and make me weak
never felt love until you touched me
healed me
i have never loved anything more or could
thanks to God for you and your love

EMPOWER

stay strong
stay fit
stay sharp in mind
believe in cruelty
trust and honour the kind
shine your light
knock on doors
if no one answers
it was not yours
keep moving
keep loving
keep fighting a good fight
even the blind can see some light
focus
drishti
concentrate
aware
awaken

BREAK THE CHAINS

sometimes you meet on your feet in love
feeling each other's heartbeat
sometimes we're not open
to choose the whitest rose
some people hang a heart wrapped in chains
around their fist so strong
hanging on
hanging on
until we see
a new beginning
you realize you were loved
you never met the beauty in you
choices guide lanterns of light
spirits we meet through the night
love with everyone
shades of the soul
love is all around

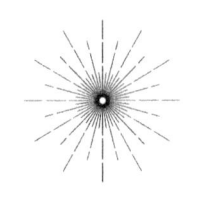

MAY YOU ALWAYS

shimmering
my love
begin this journal as you began your journey
bright-eyed and full of possibility
you were never the station my love
you are the sparkly train
may you always have your sense of wonder
may you always create vast dreams
pack your soul full of love and rainbows
it's in believing that we achieve
may you always land among illuminated stars
reflecting your gorgeous shimmer
your intentions are of goodness
your heart is full of truth
your hands are full of caring fun and youth
you're so much more than you'll ever know
your friendship a gift as crisp fallen snow

ONENESS

confusion of oneness
not the you or the me
a universal love
energy
earth and wind
fire and water
never the same
never separate
stars and animals
smiles and tears
emotions infinite
oneness is

PRESENCE

book of dreams
waves of glory
infinity the unknown story
tunnels
caves
humans as slaves
cascading grass
lifts the face
sky blue tears
crystal to cheeks
love of the world
kisses your feet

DEVOTION

let go my shattered dreams
let go my poison perfection
let go my silent screams
take from me my past
guide me through my dreams
show me the mountains i must face
let me conquer
destroy them with grace
give me wings when i sink down low
let my life finally grow
i am ready
i am here
angels let me
let go

HEARTACHE AND BUTTERFLIES

it's heartache and butterflies
tears bless my heart
times have changed
missing what was
when was the last time
how did it escape

butterflies thank moments
were you ever here
butterflies can't imagine
life without you near
this is how the story goes

heartache fights the tides
the strength of wind will blow
stop the wheels of time
to hold you by my side
just for one last kiss
the night electric
we both felt it
just for one last touch
so i could know it was the last

heartache and butterflies
are never in control
life moves us forward
we have the choice to flow
i sit on stormy seas
inside voices plead
no one to hear
no one seems near
just heartache and butterflies
waiting for flowers to appear

SHINE

i don't have tools
don't know if i'd come back
you don't know
you're a rock star

ulterior motives
hidden by smiles
a victim already
malevolent maliciousness
a faulty need
a hole to fill
it's not your job to hold them up
make them believe
in dreams
by being who they want
not who you are
rock star
fear lights them up
they love because they want you
to do and be their way
they'll never grow
nor stand their own
false fantasy
you think you make them happy

based on your acting skill
life is too short
you don't know
you're a rock star

shine your star
from the inside
drive for hours
have to lie
being honest is not your vibe
how can you thrive
believe in what you feel inside
drive for hours being you
find the courage to walk uncertain
life lies ahead
i believe
i see you
feel you
the world needs you
you're a rock star

old paths old patterns
yield old results
you know where they end
you can't rewrite
you can transcend
or the end won't be different
it's hard to change
and you're gifted
talented
disciplined
even harder for them
don't believe the trickster
saying you need them to survive
don't believe them
reach goals
learn skills
catch thrills
light the spark
create

see
dream
feed what you crave
nothing tastes so sweet
as conquering your own defeat
no one gets far
dragging their feet
worn paths of the past
honour your soul
with trust rewards win
it's light we're afraid of
you're a rock star
you're more than you think
rock star

FOCUS

i may always have that piece
that's dark
i've been scared
life made its mark
what you focus on expands
notice holding others' hands
unconscious spark of the past
they'll float in when i'm having
a blast
people or places i've been
i see and get them all
i'm loving to gain
notice good moments
absorb the earth's core
reflect the lighter side
behind my eyes and heart
believing achieving doing good
deeds with pride
acknowledge the kindness
dark and light
they stand side by side
choose what you see
your power is
inside

STARLIGHT

shining bright through the clouds
shining bright through me
light is what i believe
what i feel what i see
darkness all around me
i shine like the moon
moving clouds passing soon
my friend reminds
my earthly valentine
forever love
forever mine
thine in space not time
valentine
shining bright through the clouds
love
light
as we allow
burn bright this night
forever now

ELEVATE

you don't need to be fixed
you've got too much distraction
i need you to sit
know i'm enough
not on your phone
looking for more stuff
opening gates for opinion
and lack
i've been there before
i'm covering those tracks
i'd rather be alone
owning my truths
'til i'm put in the ground
i'll stand tall
on solid ground
no negativity
taking me down
again
and again
beginning
end

MASTER

sands of time
warriors journey
transcending mine
feeling through souls
opportunity grown
heart and love skills
relationships reflect
practice
insight
trust
belief
freedom you can share
with kindness they'll touch
momentum
spirited awakening
heart and soul lifted
higher vibration
dimensions within
infinite
cosmic connection
within

MORTALITY

along the ride your chair sits inside
scattered times of yours in mine
senseless thoughts of places you've been
trapped inside an endless dream

a valley high and rivers shallow
step inside and feel the swallow
taste the air and bite the breath
fear nothing on your path through death

between your thoughts you turn your cheek
take a pause and feel the heat
circle your gift and lift the tone
feel your power unlock the throne

a valley high and rivers sweet
step inside beyond defeat
feel the air and bite the breath
fear nothing on your path through death
take a breath to catch the kiss

reveal your swords of ancient chests
release the pain and victim's role
take a pause and gain control

a valley high and rivers shallow
step inside and feed your soul
taste the air and swallow each breath
reveal it all on your path to death

HIGH

we hang out together
way too much fun
we get high
i want to get higher
never come down
with you
feel so good

i don't see you as much
i want you so bad
waves crash and land
til we're found on the cloud
i want to get higher
with you

your tender lips
your eyes when you're inside
do we miss moments
being so high
can we get higher
and never come down

missing moments
my own discomfort I realize
could it be my demise
what you saw with your eyes
from the depths of my soul
i apologize

moments i'm missing
missing your touch
your touch got me through so much
the hours
the moments
touching with you

i'm sad i've missed moments
maybe chances too
i don't want anymore
missed moments with you
i want to get higher
never come down
with you

WITHIN

i see through
and just in case
i witness love in every place
in each vessel's swollen thought
i hear only peace
whispering justice taught
see and feel and bless my eyes
taste your breath and open wide
rivals bitter sweet repair
i heal and love your angel's glare
in deepened pockets
stuffed torn and wide
through baskets split
leftover pride
i touch and taste a marvel of thought
i penetrate ears and eyes
with thought
the inversion sounds a screeching blare
sirens bask in heavens wear
attire knitted tight
you clench and worm
desire is pulled and cast in fume
vapour too tense exploding in heat
i heal your blood

not bitterness
sweet
i heal to depths of blindness within
i heal today and all past sin
to touch and feel
a wondrous state
to kneel and clutch the heavens gate
healing time as broken wings
in hearts we stand and only sing
forgotten soldiers broken vests
healing within our nature's nest
piquing to each luscious bloom
taste each step of breathing room
i am the cleanser washing through
i am the love
hidden in you

LETTING GO

i forgive myself
for walls i've built
sorry for the pain
too long holding the freight train
thought i was strong
for hanging on
never feeling the strength
just in knowing it
true strength is
letting go

IF

if i should wade in shallow waters
my hope would be to feel your touch
if i should buckle with weakness
hope to soar in your arms
if i should be blinded by fear
hope to feel pure love
if i stretch beyond my peace
hope to be held back
feel the feelings
i need to feel
become the feelings
release the feelings
breathe
awesome breath
if i should falter
fall with pain
hope i want to be again
intense and bold
an exquisite taste
hope to love
live in faith
if i would doubt a single act
pray for light to cross my path
hope for times

fear's nest resides
in instant lullaby
if i could sing on mountain tops
my hope would be to listen
if i could chose one potent stroke
my hope would be to hear

ANGEL DUST

angel dust
on pink cheeks
love in the colour green
reflections of truth
dancing mirror of tears
innocent youth
frozen in season
destined for dreams
love never dies

LOVING MOTHER

sweet soul
bless you
sleep peacefully
a quiet space
angel's breast
rest your feet
a loving retreat
soul of your mother
retreat
retreat
listen
hear the heartbeat
feel as one
daughters and sons
loving mother
you are one
all wounds undone
love

LEADING LIGHTS

it's uncertain times
no rhyme or reason
it's a time
fraught with change
it's a time
for a new season
this journey isn't out there
this journey is within
the leading lights are dim
the leading lights within

NOWHERE LEFT TO HURT

once the mind is made
there's only moving forward
when bridges are burned
you've nowhere left to hurt
nowhere left to burn
taken every turn
all you've done is learn
it's growth
growth in its finest
the finest place to grow love
i've gotta find the words
to tell you how i feel
gotta find the words
so you can know its real
not the stories you've embedded
i'm not the stories you feel
my heart burns
my soul real
your stories are from other girls
you've touched their curls
that's not me
days like these
i wish it was me you loved
you've been shattered

you've been torn
it's not her crown i wear
my heart space is soft
my words seldom heard
nowhere left to hurt

DANCING LOVE

feelings surrounding me
finding their way
through gaping gazes
delicately wounded
perspiration oozing
meets vials of prescription
viral thoughts
what why how where
and want

feelings crowning me
piercing the fog
coveting desire
masking conscious
creativity destructive
sensuality meeting passion with a kiss
demon dragon strings
heart flooded
free falling deeper
dancing love
drizzling fires of dark desires
mercy glands transpires
peace
wholeness fallen upon thy foot
glory
warm soothing sun
anticipation
spring mountain peaks
tender rose petal
loving

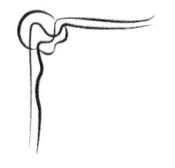

THE DANCER

final moments close to the clouds
swallowing lumps
looking at shadows
grasping the peace
the final day of the full moon

now is for thanks from God
and angels
now is for
strength

i have seen the dancer
in candles incense clouds flags
blades of grass trees leaves
ripples on the lake

i have lit and touched and seen
angels
no mistake
i have laughed and cried
lived and died
all in a moon cycle

i can see i can be

i can write i can fight
for only love
i saw doors open
felt the fear
trusted the universe
love and angels were near
never be the same

thanks for the glory in me God
thank you angels
for all you've done
now is for courage
strength
letting go
truth trust and faith
courage to keep moving
strength to move
to be
to trust
and let go
leave my love in angel's care
let go of me
my thoughts
my actions
beliefs
my beloved twin
all else i thought was me

i can be free
knowing who i am
truth to those i created
truth is understanding
faith is for survival
to sing and shine
faith in the universe
that brought me this day
that i am always okay
that i can be who God intended
faith
that my love and i will always be

one day light the world
together
faith that we will always be
together

i am in my dreams
i am where love is
no more fear
thank you God for lifting me
angels keep me always
hold me if i weep
please work your magic
miracles in my life
carry me when my wings are dry
remind me always
i can fly
i have seen the dancer

LOTUS POSE

lotus pose
no one knows
freeing yourself
the mind it blows
lotus pose
no one knows
it is what it is
a thankless sin
lotus pose
to hold your toes
or let it seep right in
no one knows
lotus pose
the smoke that burns within

I ASK YOU

it's always been a dream
i've held it deep within
to write the greatest love song
that ever did exist
with passion erupting
malnourished inside
it's your face that i captured
as i dare uncover and hide

and i ask you if you know how much
i love you
i ask
i need to know
some things are never said
how much i love you
you should know
my passion explodes in outstretched arms
grasping what it is

i feel
thoughts of you piercing
through me
i am real
because i have you
what you are to me
you don't know

and i ask if you know how much
i love you
i ask
i need to know
some things are never said
but take my love
as you go

your spirit as a wave comes crashing
through my mind
your presence is a gift from God
as perishable as mine
your laughter is the music
dancing in my soul
your touch heals every wound
i can't control

and i ask if you know how much
i love you
i ask
i need to know
some things just should be said
before the angels
bring us home

i'll tell you how much i love you
though its more than you could know
it's what wakes me up each morning
gives me strength
and peace to grow

so, take how much i love you
and hold it in your heart
and as the angels guide you home
we shall never live apart

SOULS COLLIDE

clouds of bliss as souls collide
avalanches of enchanted emotions
coming in waves we ride
we suffer
sweet will soon be sweeter
communicate, validate, appreciate
love you have today
light on darkest days
hearts held by wings of love
frequencies soared above
every day is the game
a brilliant pillar
empire of strength
feeding flames
some souls collide

STRETCHING

floating space
peaceful grace
wings are clouds
that i embrace
trees that taste
the earth and sky
clouds tall parents
branches reach
communicating clouds
trees that teach
water drowns
as cleansing fuel
heat of the light
a silent pull
that blinds the fool
stretching the eye between
strong trees
free birds
grazing
growing
blooming is to be

MIDDLE PATH

not to meet you
here to teach you
healing souls of hidden wounds
be pure, open
light is the way
float freely
silence, quiet down
nothing outside will fill your soul
close your eyes, feel
let your light shine through
every moment, love
you will feel me there
guiding you to be who you are
break the shackles, carve the stone
walk the path of scary, unknown
that dimension i'm breathing on
listen, chase
your heart, song
total eclipse
poet and poem
feelings vs known
wetness of tears
light through fears

do the work
choose the hard way
you can transform the middle path
once you set adrift the easy raft

AFFIRM

i am loving
i am loved
i am powerful
i am joy
i am peace
i am strength
i am courage
i am determination
i am love

DREAM

in the hollow of the dream
feel the relentless scream
dying to the end
you've already seen
in thought
in prayer
the world has left you
naked
bare

in the hollow of the dream
you wish you scream
to an audience
out of sight
someone appearing black as night
as you wish
you close
naked
bare

you dream the hollow dream
though no one is there
alone in the silent
still of the fright

you repeat your episode
night after night
with thought and prayer
since no one is there

in the hollow of the dream
you twist and scream
unaware and bare
nothing as it seems
you tear a wet stream
in the hollow of your dream

the hollow of your dream
you could not see
as you are wrapped in a warmth
of piercing wings
naked and raw
you create this stream…
into a world of blessing
you have yet to dream

DADDY

if i had to write to see you
i'd write across mountains
high winds, cold snow
i'd write to mountain tops, through valleys below
i'd write my whole life long
oh daddy, i could...
i'd write just to hold you
i promise i would
i'd write for a phone call
i'd write for your advice
i'd write to hear you say my name
once probably twice
knowing us
i'd write to hear your laugh your racist jokes
i'd write to those days back in the seventies
you were killing me with players light smoke
i'd write to watch you with my sister
i know how much you miss her
i'd write back in time to feel your hand in mine
you've guided me to write these lines...
i smell your breath
i see your hair
days are hardest when i don't feel you there

i'm writing for you daddy, high up on a plane
writing to you, so you know i care
i miss you and i love you
always be there

YOU ARE FINE

that light inside
so far away
head above water
though you felt you had no air
you can see
i was always there
we are the light of the world
each other
all i want to see
your angelic shine
will touch the world
as it has mine
this is your way
breathe
love
you are fine

MIRACLES

even imprisoned
gifts toss miracles of light
through ironclad walls
the angel smells the freedom
and flies towards the fear
wings of confidence
the power to heal
the power to feel
sharing dilutes the acidic burn
and light now fills the void
no holes in the ocean
we're born again
alive

I KNOW

first i feel you
blessing between my toes
then you hug me
as only i know
i wait in the moment
breathing in slow
i wade through your movement
as only i know
each step towards
your inner peace
each wave that wraps
my body in heat
each tingle as you kiss my eyes
each dolphin's gentle lullaby
that heals all wounds
mustered with fear
that soothes my chest
burning with fear
in hope of solitude
the wings you gave to someone new
feel your presence
tighten its grip
safer the further i slip
my eyes caress

the peace you are
i am drifting upon heaven's shore
i see the light
as only i know
and feel the God within me sow
the peace i am
i know
i know

RISE OF THE GODDESS

when i'm unhappy, i write lists
lists of what i want
like, *i need to be out on my own*
or, *i want better than this*
i deserve better
or, *i want to be pregnant*
i want motherhood.
when what i want comes in, i make a new list
i write lists of my positive qualities.
like, *i am educated, smart, beautiful, intelligent, loving, peaceful, talented, independent, ambitious, fun, funny*
i write lists of where i am emotionally
like, *i am emotionally abused, constantly tested, put down, unappreciated*
rise of the goddess equals
the force of being
universe
creation
spiritual pattern
procreation
just be and know i am
paradise equals power
to perceive perfection
wake up

give each day to God
may the universe's will be done
always begin
let go
begin again

HOLLOW OF THE TWISTED TREE

through the hollow of the twisted tree
truth will set us free
though no truth has a smiling face
truth supersedes a distinguished race
through branches of distorted thought
truth swings in tune with forget-me-not
although the valley's echo swears
truth has no ears and always dares
in through the water's crystal stare
truth lurks behind the shepherd's glare
entwined inside the mind of youth
truth's power is only that—of truth
fear of the unknown it's fear we fear
we lie to our lovers when truth is clear

through the hollow of the twisted tree
the truth will set us free

EVEN WIDER

i ponder the openness
of my sweet heart
through the delicate gaze
of the ancient tree
telling its own stories
of love, hate, loneliness, despair, and wanting
through the crooked branches
withering leaves
lie many nights of strength
nights of need
nights of me

i feel weather
place its nature
upon the breaking rotted corpse
i ponder how she never sheds or breaks
a comforting knowingness
she was created to be
to take what touches her breast naturally

i choose to shift my focus
away from crooked collapsing sticks
to find atop of her beauty
a sturdy branch
wholesome
aspiring
emerald leaves and juicy sprouts
tiny toes of innocent squirrels

i am as sturdy, strong, and beautiful
despite the weather
i smile as i feel my heart begin to open
even wider

ABOUT THE AUTHOR

Andrea Lynn Wehlann has received the Editor's Choice Award for Outstanding Achievement in Poetry by The National Library of Poetry (Canada), Honourable Mention from Illiad Press, and a Poet of Merit Award. Her poetry has been published in *The Brock Press Literary Supplement, The 1996 Blue Ribbon Collection, Portraits of Life* published by the National Library of Poetry and the International Society of Poets, and *Another Nobody: A Tribute to the Homeless by Niagara's Poets*. Andrea was a distinguished member of the International Society of Poets for more than seven years and has in the past been a member of The Canadian Theosophical Society. She's been featured in publications like Niagara Life Magazine.

Andrea is a certified Hatha Yoga teacher and owns and operates the Ganga Moon Yoga Studio in Beamsville, Ontario, Canada. With a BA in psychology from Brock University and a social services diploma from Niagara College, Andrea's work as a recognized social services worker, practitioner of first degree Usui Reiki, Brazilian Jiu Jitsu, Chi Kung, Feng Shui, and meditation round out her teaching experience.

Her dedication to spiritual healing comes from overcoming childhood, mental, physical, and emotional abuse, surviving rape and sexual assault, miscarriages and infant loss, personal experiences make her an effective healer today. The gift she strives to share with others is that she sees the world as a whole and that we are all equal parts of that whole.

Find Andrea on social media through the links below, if you're reading this on an e-reader, or by searching the platforms below using the term "Ganga Moon Yoga."

Visit her author page at https//ingeniumbooks.com/andrea-lynn-wehlann.